BY JAMES S. KELLEY

THE ATLANTIC DIVISION

THE BOSTON CELTICS

THE NEW JERSEY NETS

THE NEW YORK KNICKS

THE PHILADELPHIA 76ERS

THE TORONTO RAPTORS

Published in the United States of America by
The Child's World® • 1980 Lookout Drive
Mankato, MN 56003-1705
800-599-READ • www.childsworld.com

ACKNOWLEDGEMENTS

The Child's World®: Mary Berendes,
Publishing Director

The Design Lab: Kathleen Petelinsek,
Design and Page Production

Manuscript consulting and photo research by
Shoreline Publishing Group LLC.

PHOTOS

Cover: Corbis
Interior photos: Corbis: 4, 7, 17, 22, 25;
Reuters: 8, 10, 13, 14, 18, 21, 26, 28, 30, 32

**LIBRARY OF CONGRESS
CATALOGING-IN-PUBLICATION DATA**

Kelley, James S., 1960–

The Atlantic division / by James S. Kelley.

   p. cm. — (Above the rim)

Includes bibliographical references and index.

ISBN 978-1-59296-981-4
(library bound: alk. paper)

1. National Basketball Association—History—
Juvenile literature. 2. Basketball—East (U.S.)—
History—Juvenile literature. I. Title. II. Series.

GV885.515.N37K44 2008

796.323'640973—dc22   2007034761

CONTENTS

*On the cover: High-flying Vince Carter
gave the steadily improving New Jersey
Nets a new scoring force.*

INTRODUCTION

The Atlantic Division of the National Basketball Association (NBA) is a little bit like the starting five of a very good basketball team. The Boston Celtics are the all-star center of this "team," with an all-time NBA-record 16 NBA championships. The Celtics have boasted some of the greatest players ever. Playing a very strong power forward on the Atlantic team are the New York Knicks, another old and successful club. At the small forward spot is the Philadelphia 76ers, who have had some success, but not as much national fame.

At the guard spots are a pair of younger teams, the New Jersey Nets and Toronto Raptors.

All together this starting five has won more than 20 NBA titles and featured a parade of superstars of all ages. The only question will be how to get them all on the court at the same time! Read on to learn the history of this outstanding NBA division.

CHAPTER ONE

THE BOSTON CELTICS

Bob Cousy's ballhandling skills helped change the way basketball was played. His pinpoint passes made his teammates better.

The Celtics have made history almost from their first season in 1946. In 2007, however, they grabbed headlines not for winning, but for making a trade. To the long and impressive line of Celtics' superstars, add the name of Kevin Garnett.

The Celtics traded a record five players and two draft picks to land the 10-time All-Star from Minnesota. Garnett will join fellow all-stars Ray Allen and Paul Pierce to create a very powerful front line starting in the 2007–08 season.

That trio will have big shoes to fill in Celtics' history, however. Not long after their founding as a member of the Basketball Association of America (one of the groups that formed the NBA in 1947), the Celtics soon became the most dominant **franchise** in basketball history. The key came in 1950, when the Celtics hired Red Auerbach as coach. Auerbach quickly found a center in Ed Macauley. Then, the Celtics got a little lucky. In a drawing to choose players from a team that had folded, the Celtics drew rookie Bob Cousy. At the time, he was the least-desirable choice of the players available. Eventually, Cousy made it into the Hall of Fame. His pinpoint passing and fancy ball-handling helped change the way the game is played.

Auerbach continued to add pieces to the puzzle, including shooting guard Bill Sharman and forward Frank Ramsey, and Boston became a regular **playoff** participant. The big breakthrough came in 1956–57. First, the Celtics selected Holy Cross forward Tom Heinsohn in the draft. The team then traded Macauley

Each year, the NBA Coach of the Year is given the Red Auerbach Award in honor of the many accomplishments of the long-time Celtics' coach.

and rookie Cliff Hagen to St. Louis in exchange for center Bill Russell.

After signing Heinsohn and Russell, everything fell into place. Heinsohn was a solid forward and the NBA's Rookie of the Year in 1956–57. Russell was a dominant defensive player and rebounder who went on to win five NBA Most Valuable Player (MVP) awards. Over the next 13 seasons, the Celtics ruled the NBA like no other team before or since.

Boston won its first championship in 1956–57 with a thrilling 125–123 victory over the St. Louis Hawks in double overtime in Game 7 of the **NBA Finals**. St. Louis avenged that defeat in 1958, but the Celtics bounced back in 1958–59 to win the first of an unprecedented eight consecutive championships.

Over the years, the names of the players changed, but the Celtics maintained a **legacy** of success. Cousy retired after the club's fifth consecutive title in 1962–63, but talented forward John Havlicek arrived the same season. Auerbach stepped down as coach after the eighth straight title in 1965–66, but remained as the team's general manager. The new coach was Russell, who continued to play as well. (An important historical note is that when he was named to replace Auerbach, Russell became the first African-American coach of any major professional sports team.)

Even though the Celtics have featured stars such as Russell, Cousy, and Bird, longtime guard John "Hondo" Havlicek is the team's all-time leading scorer. He tossed in 26,395 points in his own Hall of Fame career.

After leading the team to back-to-back titles in 1968–69, Russell retired as both player and coach and with a spot in history as one of the game's all-time greats.

Center Dave Cowens helped the team win a pair of titles in the 1970s, while the 1980s belonged to Larry Bird. A three-time league MVP, Bird teamed with center Robert Parish and forward Kevin McHale to lead Boston to three more championships. Bird was another in the Celtics' line of all-time greats. Not blessed with speed or tremendous size, he made up for it with hard work and creativity. He was also a deadly outside shooter and stunning passer. His on-court battles with Lakers superstar Magic Johnson helped make the NBA more popular than ever.

In a 1985 victory over Atlanta, Larry Bird set the Celtics' single-game scoring record when he poured in 60 points.

Bird and company led Boston to titles in 1981, 1984, and 1986. After losing in the 1987 Finals, and with the retirement of Bird in 1993, Boston entered a very low period. By 1996–97, the Celtics reached bottom, when the club's 15–67 record was the worst in its history.

The next year, however, the team drafted guard Paul Pierce. By 2001–02, when he averaged a career-best 26.2 points per game, Pierce was one of the top players in the NBA. Then the Celtics won the Atlantic Division title in 2004–05. It was their first division championship in 13 years.

Finally, the big trade in 2007 set up the Celtics for a possible return to their glory years. Pierce remains one of the NBA's all-around talents, while Allen is a sharp-shooting guard. Garnett, or "KG" as he is known, is a powerful inside force, excellent at both rebounding and finding open men with passes. Together, the trio have created basketball excitement in Boston again. Now, if they can just find a way to win championship number 17…

Kevin Garnett joined the Celtics in 2007, joining fellow All-Stars Paul Pierce and Ray Allen.

CHAPTER TWO

THE NEW JERSEY NETS

Thanks in large part to the play of outstanding guard Jason Kidd, the New Jersey Nets have been one of the NBA Eastern Conference's top teams in recent years. For Nets' fans, the success has been a long time coming. They had only occasionally shown

Jason Kidd's leadership and passing ability helped the Nets win two Eastern Conference championships.

anything near the team's great seasons in the mid-2000s.

The wait for this success began when the club first started play in the American Basketball Association (ABA) in 1967. That new league wanted a great team in New York, the nation's largest city. Instead, it got a squad of journeymen and **semipros** who played in a converted **armory** in Teaneck, New Jersey, and went by the name the New Jersey Americans. The next year, the club changed its name to the New York Nets and moved to Long Island. The team eventually played in five different arenas before landing for good in New Jersey in 1977—and taking the name New Jersey Nets.

The Nets were the ABA's worst team at 17–61 in 1969. They acquired their first star in 1970, when they signed flashy, high-scoring forward Rick Barry. One year later, the team was in the ABA Finals. Though they lost that series to the Indiana Pacers, they won fans and attention in the New York City area.

Barry was gone the next year, and the club quickly fell back to its old ways. However, a new star emerged in 1973 to finally lead the Nets to the top. Few players in NBA history were as exciting to watch—or as hard to defend—as the legendary Julius "Dr. J." Erving. In his first year with the Nets, he led the ABA with

The Americans became the Nets in 1968 to rhyme with two other New York teams: football's Jets and baseball's Mets.

a 27.4 points-per-game average, and they won the league championship. They won again in 1976, the last year before the ABA **merged** with the NBA.

The move to the NBA proved painful for the Nets. Erving left the team at the same time, and the double blow led to several years with terrible records. Throughout the 1980s and 1990s, the Nets annually had some of the worst teams in the entire league. They did have some good players—Buck Williams became the club's all-time leading scorer and rebounder, for example. But they made the playoffs only once, in 1984. They also suffered tragedy in 1993, when popular guard Drazen Petrovic was killed in a car accident at the age of 28.

In the new century (and millennium), things began to turn around. In 2001–02, the Nets had their best NBA record ever at 52–30 and won their first Atlantic Division title. They made it all the way to the NBA Finals before losing there to the Los Angeles Lakers. Kidd was the key, and he made high-scoring forward Kenyon Martin even better with pinpoint passes.

Undaunted by that defeat, New Jersey won 49 games in 2002–03 and again reached the NBA Finals. The Nets played well, but lost in six games to the San Antonio Spurs.

In the 1990s, high-flying Kenyon Martin led the Nets. His great leaping ability made him a force on offense and as a rebounder on defense.

Buck Williams was a star forward who earned three All-Star selections for the Nets in the 1980s. He is the franchise's all-time leading scorer and rebounder.

Vince Carter's scoring touch helped turn the Nets from a so-so team to one of the East's best.

With Kidd earning his third consecutive All-Star selection and Martin his first, the Nets won the Atlantic Division again the following season. But after an easy four-game sweep of the Knicks in the opening round, New Jersey's title hopes

The Nets missed the playoffs in their inaugural season when they had to forfeit a showdown with the Kentucky Colonels for the last spot because their home arena was in unplayable condition.

were dashed again, this time by eventual-champion Detroit. The Pistons rallied from a three-games-to-two deficit to win an exciting seven-game series.

New Jersey's three-year run atop the Atlantic Division abruptly ended in 2004–05, when Martin left the club after becoming a **free agent**. All-star swingman Vince Carter was acquired early in the season from Toronto and averaged 27.5 points per game for the Nets, but the club struggled, winning as many games as it lost. Still, a dramatic four-game winning streak to end the **regular season** lifted the Nets to a 42–40 record and into the playoffs.

They made it five straight division titles in 2005–06, with Carter and Kidd continuing to lead the team. In 2006–07, they finished second in the division, but had a great playoff run, upsetting the Raptors in the first round and nearly knocking off the LeBron James-led Cavaliers in the second.

Nets fans now expect a playoff run every season, and that's a far cry from running from arena to arena in the team's early years.

CHAPTER THREE

THE NEW YORK KNICKS

The New York Knicks (short for Knickerbockers, a nickname for colonial New Yorkers from Holland) play in the nation's biggest city before some of the NBA's most loyal fans. However, they have only rewarded those fans with a title twice. Though one came thanks to one of the NBA's bravest moments, the Knicks remain a club that seems to often come close, but not quite make it to the top.

The Knicks began their almost-but-not-quite history in 1946 as a team in the Basketball Association of America, one of the leagues that formed the NBA. The Knicks advanced to the NBA Finals three consecutive years (1951, 1952, and 1953), only to come up short each time. They were led by Hall of Fame coach Joe Lapchick and All-Stars Carl Braun and Dick McGuire.

The next decade or so featured little success. By the late 1960s, however, the team had rebounded. Center Willis Reed joined in 1964, and Red Holzman was named coach in 1967. Guard Walt "Clyde" Frazier and forward Bill Bradley joined Reed. In 1970, the Knicks finally broke

After leaving the NBA, Bill Bradley was elected a U.S. Senator from New Jersey and later ran for the Democratic Presidential nomination.

The Knicks of the 1950s, here goofing off for a photographer, reached the NBA Finals three times without winning.

through with their first NBA championship, beating the Lakers in seven games.

Game 7 of that series included one
of the most famous moments in NBA
history. Reed had suffered a torn thigh
muscle in Game 5 and missed the next
game. Without the Knicks' 6-foot-9, 235-
pound center clogging the middle, the
Lakers' Wilt Chamberlain had his way in
Game 6, scoring 45 points and hauling

down 27 rebounds. Los Angeles breezed to a 135–113 **rout** that tied the series.

As the teams warmed up in New York's Madison Square Garden for Game 7, Reed stayed in the locker room for

Patrick Ewing was the first player taken in the 1985 NBA Draft. He had a big impact, helping turn the Knicks into winners again.

How did the Knicks get Ewing? They won a lottery. The bottom seven teams in the NBA earn a chance to get the top pick in the NBA Draft. The more games a team loses, the better their chances. The Knicks were the lucky team in 1985.

treatment. No one thought he would be able to play. But fans and the Lakers were stunned when he limped onto the court shortly before tip-off. The fans' roars rattled the Garden's roof. Though clearly hobbled, Reed quickly made a pair of jumpers to open the scoring in the game. He left the game soon after, but he didn't need to play again. The Knicks were energized by his bravery and rode that emotion and the fans' excitement to a 113–99 win and their first NBA title.

In 1973, the Knicks won their second NBA title, defeating the Lakers again. They were aided by the addition of flashy guard Earl "The Pearl" Monroe. He joined Frazier to make up one of the NBA's best-ever backcourts (the two guards together are called by that name). Another key player was forward Dave DeBusschere, whose fierce defensive play was a perfect match for the offense of fellow forward Bradley.

By the mid-1970s, the Knicks' run was over. They had several losing seasons before bottoming out with a last-place finish in 1984–85. Then their fortunes turned again. They won the right to the first pick in the 1985 NBA Draft. The Knicks chose Georgetown center Patrick Ewing and kicked off a long period of success. Led by the dominant center (and for a while by former Lakers' championship coach Pat Riley), New York earned 14 consecutive playoff appearances from 1988 to 2001, three division titles, and two Eastern Conference championships. They made the 1994 NBA Finals, but lost to Houston in a seven-game series. In 1999, they squeaked into the playoffs, but after a series of upsets were in the Finals again. However, they lost to San Antonio in five games. Through all this success, the big prize—an NBA championship—eluded the Knicks.

After Ewing left in 2000, they made the playoffs only once through 2007 and their last winning record came in 2000–2001. To make matters worse, in that playoff appearance in 2004, they were swept by the New Jersey Nets. That other team from the New York area was on the rise even as the Knicks were heading the other way. Plus, that series loss brought big changes to the Knicks. Former star NBA guard Isiah Thomas was hired as president of basketball operations and revamped the club. Thomas hired Hall of Famer Larry Brown to take over as coach. While the play of flashy guard Stephon Marbury was a highlight, the changes didn't help much, however. Over the next few years, the Knicks were among the NBA's worst teams. For a city that had enjoyed such success over the years, it was a tough blow.

Eddy Curry used his long reach and powerful inside game to lead the Knicks in scoring in 2006–07, averaging 19.8 points per game.

Eddy Curry's powerful inside game has been a bright spot for the Knicks in recent seasons.

CHAPTER FOUR

THE PHILADELPHIA 76ERS

Dolph Schayes (4) was a franchise star from 1949 through 1964. Here, he tangles with fellow big man Wilt Chamberlain while with Syracuse.

The Philadelphia 76ers have featured some of the NBA's biggest stars since they began play in 1949. However, all those stars have not aligned to make much continued success, though they have produced periods of greatness. Since joining

In 1948, the National Basketball League and Basketball Association of America came together to form the National Basketball Association, now known worldwide as the NBA.

the NBA in 1949–1950, the club has won three league titles. Only the Celtics, Lakers, and Bulls have won more.

The team's first title came while the team played in Syracuse, New York, and was called the Nationals. The Nationals were one of six National Basketball League teams that helped to form today's NBA in 1949. The Nats' big star was forward Dolph Schayes. At 6-foot-8, Schayes was one of the first big men who also had a **deft** shooting touch. With Schayes leading the way, the Nationals won 51 of 64 regular-season games. They advanced to the first NBA Finals in 1949 before losing to the Minneapolis Lakers (that team later moved to Los Angeles, of course). The Lakers foiled Syracuse's hopes again in 1954, but the Nationals won the 1955 title with a seven-game victory over Fort Wayne in the finals.

The club relocated to Philadelphia for the 1963–64 season and was renamed the 76ers.

Two years later, Philadelphia made big news by acquiring 7-foot-1 center Wilt Chamberlain from the Warriors. In 1961–62, Chamberlain had averaged an unbelievable 50.4 points and 25.7 rebounds a game for the Warriors, who were then in Philadelphia. In a game against New York that season, he scored a record 100 points. He is still the only player to reach that mark in an NBA game, and many of his other scoring records remain unchallenged. For all his great talent, however, many people said that Chamberlain couldn't win a championship. That changed in 1966–67 with the 76ers. Teamed with fellow future Hall of Famers Hal Greer and Billy Cunningham, Chamberlain helped lead the Sixers to a 68–13 record during the regular season. After ending Boston's eight-year run as NBA champions in the Eastern finals, the 76ers defeated Chamberlain's old team, the Warriors, in six games to win the title.

Chamberlain played only one more year with the 76ers before being traded to Los Angeles, and the 76ers won just nine games in 1972–73. But the club didn't stay down long and soon added its next big superstar in 1976, when Julius Erving was acquired from the New York Nets. "Dr. J" made an immediate impact, playing every game his first season with Philadelphia and helping the team win 50 regular-season games and its first Atlantic Division championship.

The 76ers reached the NBA Finals that year, only to lose to the Portland Trail Blazers in six games. With Erving leading the way, Philadelphia won conference championships again in 1979–1980 and 1981–82, only to have powerful Los Angeles Lakers teams end their run at each title.

Why was Dr. J so great? His amazing leaping ability was one reason. He once took off from the free-throw line, flew through the air, and finally dunked the basketball into the hoop.

Finally in 1982–83, Philadelphia broke through. After roaring to a 65–17 record during the regular season, the 76ers were unstoppable in the playoffs. They won 12 of 13 postseason games, including a four-game sweep of the Lakers in the finals to win the league championship. That team featured yet another big name—and big guy—center Moses

The Doctor is in . . . the basket! Julius "Dr. J." Erving brought flair and style to the NBA. His all-around skills also helped bring the 76ers three conference titles.

Malone, who was named the NBA MVP that year.

Another famous star joined the 76ers the next season, Charles Barkley. Though not a very graceful player, he used strength and determination to become one of the league's top players.

Not surprisingly, Wilt Chamberlain holds the 76ers' single-game record for points in a game. He scored 68 in a game against Chicago in 1967.

He was named to the All-NBA first team four times through 1991.

The 76ers have not won the title since then, but they have reached the play-offs a few times. That includes a stretch of five consecutive years in the postseason from 1998–99 through 2002–03, all under Hall of Fame coach Larry Brown (who went on to lead Detroit to the NBA title in 2003–04).

Allen Iverson was another in the long line of the 76ers' shooting stars. He was the NBA MVP in 2000–01 and guided the 76ers to the NBA Finals. He led the league in scoring that season. However, one hot scorer was not enough. Philly made the playoffs only one more time through 2007. Iverson was traded to the Denver Nuggets early in the 2006–07 season, leaving the 76ers in search of a new star to help them make it back to the top.

Basketball fans in Toronto, Canada, waited almost half a century for pro basketball to come back to their city. Finally, the Toronto Raptors joined the NBA in 1995 as an expansion team and have given their patient fans lots to cheer for.

The Raptors may be a dozen years old, but basketball in Toronto goes back to 1946. That's when the Toronto Huskies played their one and only season in the old Basketball Association of America. The sport was played at the high school and college levels, and Canada boasted a fine national team. However, there was no pro team until the NBA announced that basketball would return to Toronto. It granted the city an expansion team, set to begin play in the 1995–96 season.

To help kick off the Raptors' first season in the league, the NBA Draft was actually held at the famous SkyDome in Toronto in 1995.

Toronto fans entered a contest to choose the team's name and colors. The winning name was Raptors, after a dinosaur in the movie *Jurassic Park*. Dozens of dinosaur species have been discovered in Canada; the country even has a place called Dinosaur Provincial Park. Isiah Thomas, a Hall of Fame point guard from the Detroit Pistons, was put in charge of building the team roster. Canadian fans

Marcus Camby, battling Michael Jordan here, was an early star for the Raptors before moving on to play for the Knicks and Nuggets.

One guess how Vince "Air Canada" Carter got his nickname . . . Carter electrified fans with his soaring dunks.

The Raptors set a less-than-wonderful mark in 2006, when they allowed Kobe Bryant of the Lakers to score 81 points, the second-most ever in one NBA game.

hungry for NBA basketball snapped up season tickets at a rapid rate.

Like any expansion team, the Raptors struggled at first, and they won just 21 games in their first season. Canadian fans did get to enjoy the play of young stars like Damon Stoudamire and Marcus Camby. In 1999, another young Raptor, Vince Carter, won the Rookie of the Year award. The future looked bright.

The 1999–2000 season held several firsts for Toronto. Carter, nicknamed "Air Canada" for his high-flying dunking ability, became the first Raptor to appear in an NBA All-Star Game. His spectacular play helped lead the team to its first winning season (a 45–37 regular-season record) and into the playoffs for the first time as well. In the first NBA playoff series ever played outside the United States, the Raptors lost to the New York Knicks.

The Raptors kept roaring and made the playoffs in each of the next two seasons. In 2000–01, under Hall of Fame coach Lenny Wilkens, the Raptors won 47 regular-season games (a club record they tied in 2006–07) and finished in second place in the NBA's Central Division (they later moved to the Atlantic Division). The club then won its first postseason series, beating the mighty New York Knicks three games to two in the opening round. They moved on in the playoffs, but lost to even-

tual conference-champion Philadelphia in seven games.

Carter was hailed as one of the NBA's rising stars, and the Raptors as one of the league's up-and-coming teams. But after a third consecutive playoff appearance in 2001–02, Toronto fell back on tough times, posting losing seasons the next two years. Frustrated by the team's lack of success, Carter asked to be traded. His wish was granted early in 2004–05. Air Canada flew south to the division-rival Nets in exchange for three players and a pair of first-round draft choices.

Though the Raptors went on to win only 33 games that year, they thrilled fans with one of the highest-scoring offenses in the league. Small forward Jalen Rose led the team by averaging 18.5 points per game, and young Chris Bosh gave the team an emerging star. For the next few years, however, they didn't do much more than run in place, missing the playoffs until 2007. That year, they finally came together under coach Sam Mitchell. The Raptors tied a team record with 47 wins and finished in third place in the Eastern Conference. Perhaps more important, they won the Atlantic Division—finishing ahead of the Nets, led by their former star Vince Carter!

Mitchell earned the Red Auerbach Award as the NBA Coach of the Year. Bosh led the team with a 22.6 points-per-game average while also leading with 10.7 rebounds per game. Point guard T.J. Ford excited fans with his passing and averaged 7.9 assists per game. Though they were upset in the playoffs by the Nets, the challenge for Toronto will be to build on this recent success and try to bring the NBA title to Canada for the first time ever.

All in the family: Raptors team president (and 2007 NBA Executive of the Year) Bryan Colangelo is the son of Jerry Colangelo, owner of the Phoenix Suns.

1949
The Syracuse Nationals make their NBA debut

1967
The 76ers win the NBA title and stop Boston's string of eight consecutive championships

1959
The Celtics win the first of a record eight consecutive league titles

1970
The Knicks win their first NBA title

1940

1950

1960

1970

1946
The Boston Celtics and the New York Knicks begin play as charter members of the BAA (the forerunner to the NBA)

1967
The New Jersey Americans (now the Nets) begin play as charter members of the ABA

1963
The Nationals move from Syracuse to Philadelphia and become the 76ers

1957
Boston wins its first NBA title

1999
*The Raptors'
Vince Carter is
named Rookie
of the Year*

2003
*New Jersey
reaches
its second
consecutive
NBA Finals*

1974
*The Nets win
the first of two
ABA titles in
three seasons*

1980

1990

2000

2010

2007
*Boston trades
five players
and two draft
picks for
Minnesota star
Kevin Garnett*

1995
*Toronto
welcomes
the Raptors*

TEAM RECORDS
(through 2006–07)

TEAM	ALL-TIME RECORD	NBA TITLES (MOST RECENT)	NUMBER OF TIMES IN PLAYOFFS	TOP COACH (WINS)
Boston	2,794–1,963	16 (1985–86)	45	Red Auerbach (795)
*New Jersey	1,456–1,798	2 (1975–76)	23	Kevin Loughery (297)
New York	2,399–2,354	2 (1972–73)	38	Red Holzman (613)
Philadelphia	2,461–2,121	3 (1982–83)	43	Billy Cunningham (454)
Toronto	388–564	0	4	Lenny Wilkens (113)

*includes ABA

MEMBERS OF THE NAISMITH MEMORIAL NATIONAL BASKETBALL HALL OF FAME

BOSTON

PLAYER	POSITION	DATE INDUCTED
Nate (Tiny) Archibald	Guard	1991
Red Auerbach	Coach	1968
Dave Bing	Forward	1990
Larry Bird	Forward	1998
Walter Brown	Owner	1965
Bob Cousy	Guard	1970
Dave Cowens	Center	1991
Wayne Embry	Contributor	1999
John Havlicek	Forward	1983
Tom Heinsohn	Forward	1986
Bob Houbregs	Forward	1987
Bailey Howell	Guard	1997
K. C. Jones	Guard	1989
Sam Jones	Guard	1983
Alvin (Doggie) Julian	Coach	1967
Clyde Lovellette	Forward	1988
Ed Macauley	Center	1960
Pete Maravich	Guard	1987
Bob McAdoo	Center	2000
Kevin McHale	Forward	1999
Bill Mokray	Contributor	1965
Robert Parish	Center	2003
Andy Phillip	Guard	1961
Frank Ramsey	Guard	1981
Arnie Risen	Center	1998
Bill Russell	Center	1974
John (Honey) Russell	Coach	1964
Bill Sharman	Guard	1975
John Thompson	Coach	1999
Bill Walton	Center	1993
Dominique Wilkins	Forward-Guard	2006

NEW JERSEY

PLAYER	POSITION	DATE INDUCTED
Nate Archibald	Guard	1991
Rick Barry	Guard	1987
Larry Brown	Coach	2002
Lou Carnesecca	Coach	1992
Chuck Daly	Coach	1994
Julius Erving	Forward	1993
Bob McAdoo	Center	2000
Drazen Petrovic	Guard	2002
Willis Reed	Center	1981

NBA ATLANTIC CAREER LEADERS
(through 2006–07)

TEAM	CATEGORY	NAME (YEARS WITH TEAM)	TOTAL
Boston	Points	John Havlicek (1962–1978)	26,395
	Rebounds	Bill Russell (1956–1969)	21,620
New Jersey	Points	Buck Williams (1981–89)	10,440
	Rebounds	Buck Williams (1981–89)	7,576
New York	Points	Patrick Ewing (1985–2000)	23,665
	Rebounds	Patrick Ewing (1985–2000)	10,759
Philadelphia	Points	Hal Greer (1958–1973)	21,586
	Rebounds	Dolph Schayes (1948–1964)	11,256
Toronto	Points	Vince Carter (1998–2004)	9,420
	Rebounds	Antonio Davis (1999–2003, 2006)	2,839

NEW YORK

PLAYER	POSITION	DATE INDUCTED
Walt Bellamy	Forward	1993
Bill Bradley	Forward	1982
Hubie Brown	Contributor	2005
Dave DeBusschere	Forward	1982
Walt Frazier	Guard	1987
Harry Gallatin	Forward	1991
Tom Gola	Center	1975
Red Holzman	Coach	1986
Joe Lapchick	Forward	1966
Jerry Lucas	Forward	1979
Slater Martin	Guard	1981
Bob McAdoo	Center	2000
Al McGuire	Guard	1992
Dick McGuire	Guard	1993
Earl Monroe	Guard	1990
Willis Reed	Center	1981

PHILADELPHIA

PLAYER	POSITION	DATE INDUCTED
Charles Barkley	Forward	2006
Larry Brown	Coach	2002
Al Cervi	Guard	1984
Wilt Chamberlain	Center	1978
Billy Cunningham	Forward	1986
Julius Erving	Forward	1993
Hal Greer	Guard	1981
Alex Hannum	Forward	1998
Bailey Howell	Forward	1997
Earl Lloyd	Forward	2003
Moses Malone	Center	2001
Bob McAdoo	Center	2000
Jack Ramsay	Coach	1992
Dolph Schayes	Forward	1972
George Yardley	Forward	1996

TORONTO

PLAYER	POSITION	DATE INDUCTED
Lenny Wilkens	Guard/Coach	1989

armory—a building for housing military equipment or personnel

deft—skillful

franchise—more than just the team, it is the entire organization that is a member of a professional sports league

free agent—an athlete who has finished his contract with one team and is eligible to sign with another

legacy—something left behind by a person after their death or by an organization looking back to its past

merged—joined together

NBA Finals—a seven-game series between the winners of the NBA's Eastern and Western Conference championships

playoffs—a four-level postseason elimination tournament involving eight teams from each conference; levels include two rounds of divisional playoffs, a conference championship round, and the NBA Finals (all series are best of seven)

regular season—describes an 82-game schedule in which each of the NBA's 30 teams plays 52 games within its conference, 16 of which are within its division; a team plays two games against each team outside its conference, one at home and one away

rout—a defeat by a large margin

semipros—short for semiprofessionals; describes individuals who play a sport for money or some sort of gain, but who don't view playing the sport as their full-time occupation

Books

Gilbert, Sara. *The Story of the Toronto Raptors.* Mankato, Minn.: Creative Education, 2006.

Hareas, John. *Basketball.* New York: DK Publishers, 2005.

Keith, Ted. *Kevin Garnett (World's Greatest Athletes).* Chanhassen, Minn.: The Child's World, 2007.

Leboutillier, Nate. *The Story of the Boston Celtics.* Mankato, Minn.: Creative Education, 2006.

Leboutillier, Nate. *The Story of the New Jersey Nets.* Mankato, Minn.: Creative Education, 2006.

Rappoport, Ken. *Jason Kidd: Leader on the Court.* Berkeley Heights, N.J.: Enslow Publishers, 2004.

Stewart, Mark. *The Philadelphia 76ers.* Chicago: Norwood House Press, 2007.

Stewart, Mark and Zeysing, Matt. *The New York Knicks.* Chicago: Norwood House Press, 2006.

On the Web

Visit our Web page for lots of links about the Atlantic Division teams: *http://www.childsworld.com/links*

NOTE TO PARENTS, TEACHERS, AND LIBRARIANS: We routinely verify our Web links to make sure they are safe, active sites—so encourage your readers to check them out!

ABOUT THE AUTHORS

James S. Kelley is the pseudonym for a group of veteran sportswriters who collaborated on this series. Among them, they have worked for *Sports Illustrated*, the National Football League, and NBC Sports. They have written more than a dozen other books for young readers on a wide variety of sports.